CONDITIONS
OF THE
WOUNDED

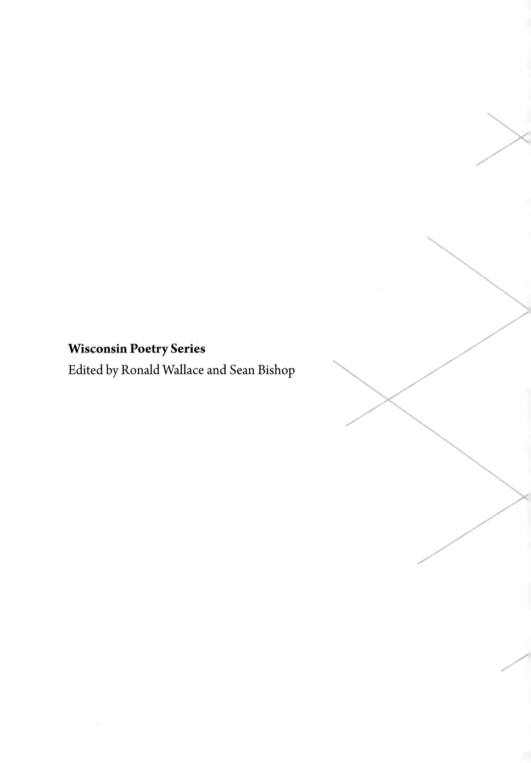

Wisconsin Poetry Series

Edited by Ronald Wallace and Sean Bishop

CONDITIONS OF THE WOUNDED

ANNA LEIGH KNOWLES

The University of Wisconsin Press

Publication of this book has been made possible, in part, through support from the Brittingham Trust.

The University of Wisconsin Press
728 State Street, Suite 443
Madison, Wisconsin 53706
uwpress.wisc.edu

Gray's Inn House, 127 Clerkenwell Road
London EC1R 5DB, United Kingdom
eurospanbookstore.com

Printed in the United States of America
This book may be available in a digital edition.

Library of Congress Cataloging-in-Publication Data

Names: Knowles, Anna Leigh, author.
Title: Conditions of the wounded / Anna Leigh Knowles.
Other titles: Wisconsin poetry series.
Description: Madison, Wisconsin : The University of
  Wisconsin Press, [2021] | Series: Wisconsin poetry series
Identifiers: LCCN 2020035436 | ISBN 9780299331443
  (paperback)
Subjects: LCGFT: Poetry.
Classification: LCC PS3611.N6858 C66 2021 | DDC
  811/.6—dc23
LC record available at https://lccn.loc.gov/2020035436

For my family

Grief strikes where love struck first.

—Anne Michaels

CONTENTS

CONDITIONS
OF THE
WOUNDED

THE BOMB SHELTER

In our backyard, a pipe rose through the ground
like a periscope. No one followed us into that hollow

girded round in steel, bent like a horseshoe raised
with us inside. Under the cool clay of the garden

our weight lay anchor. My sister and I felt the emptiness
like a pulse. Water dripped down walls and in the air,

the scent of grass and grime. We warmed the dirt
only to step out holding onto nothing but each other.

Lost sight to the sun-skinned edges of sky. Even so,
we dressed our dank stockade as though it was a sibling

we weren't allowed to speak of, in that we kept it hidden,
in that we crouched down as though root-tips yanked

at our hair. We shuffled down liters of water, cradling
the jugs under our shirts like babies waiting to be born.

The plastic against our bellies, a gift for a tilted world
without us in it. There was a hole in the ceiling for air,

an invitation, a far, damp drone. Groundwater seeped
through spade-deep grooves. Hard to say why we locked

each other inside; if only to corkscrew into our own echoes,
if only to ready the dying light of bombs we couldn't visualize.

One of us screamed up, a firmament of breath clinging
to the voiceless bulb of dark. The other sang to still the girl

beneath the green—the girl above ground
sounding as though she had seen the future and survived.

READY
THE
DYING
LIGHT,
CRY
OUT

ON LOCKDOWN

Littleton, Colorado, 1999

I'm supposed to talk about black holes.
How time bends back, everything swallowed whole.

Instead, we cluster in the corner
where Mrs. Brown sits in Dustin's desk,
blocking the entrance to the classroom.

We huddle beneath cutouts of paper planets.
Mrs. Brown tells us to get down on the floor
and we form a severed line, crossing our legs

as she rummages through the desk for anything
to read. Whatever it is, the book shakes in her hands.

She misses a few words, grips the bottom
of the chair as if to steady herself. No one mocks her.
We're too confused. Within us something pulls

and unstrings but we listen, eager for the pages
to flip and fall. Our parents arrive, cars at all angles.
Chalk flowers smudge on concrete.

They press their palms to the windows
and I can see how the bones of their hands
glow beneath their skin.

More hurry from open cars, running
with younger siblings struggling to keep up.

Amanda's mother mouths words,
points to her ears, signaling she can't hear.
We see the color gather in her cheeks.

John's father keeps his hands cupped to the sides
of his eyes, shoulders hunched as he presses his face
against the glass, eyes flitting back and forth

until they lock with his son. When he shouts John's name,
breath detonates glass. We gasp. Our parents
are forging footpaths in the hive-haunted

gardens that weave between the ferns surrounding
the main building. They gather around our rooms.
It looks like a game. Michael makes faces

at his mother. Sarah buries her face in a doll.
I worry about my older sister down the hall
stuck to a floor with the fifth graders.

Then Mrs. Brown tells us to stay down,
finish a clap game against the lime-colored walls
stacked with puzzles and our artwork.

We slap our hands together as Mrs. Brown
lowers the blinds, the sun clicking out
window by window, casting the room in shadow.

Our parents' arms tremble against the glass like webs.

BURYING THE TIME CAPSULE AT DARK
NOT LONG AFTER THE COLUMBINE
HIGH SCHOOL SHOOTING

Spring and snowmelt spread through the slush-thick meadows,
tunneling through the upper river valleys.
>   There was no climbing out of it.

Instead of tending to ourselves in that loneliness, my sister
and I gathered our once-loved things into a pathetic heap
to be buried: keychains stolen from Philips 66, homemade
>   lanyards, plastic necklaces, mood rings.

It was late night when we left our house shedding its light on wet ground.
Dropping a shovel over the fence, we hauled ourselves over
the chain-link separating the schoolyard from the back of our house,
>   crawled into a cluster of alders and dug.

It was a tequila box we lowered down like a seed,
>   measuring our steps from the trunk of an aspen
>   so years later we could reclaim what we buried.

But in the brief April mist, in the warming night
and bell-swung breeze, my sister and I are still children,
hair ruffled and nailbeds splotched
>   with each clutch and sink.

Our two shadows sunken
>   and trowel-like between billed beams of school-light.

Even then I didn't know the state flower
was the Columbine, laboring beneath the peaks,

translucent skins purpling us all.

From that day forward, we rattled inside
while the sounds of the outer world went on.

Engines revved way off. Warm wind sprang
from the curtains. Plastic bags caught
in pockets of cottonwoods. Bats nudged
high up in the rafters of the garage.

We never found it again.

Over time, our strides grew long and the box, decayed;
dredged up and ransacked from the earth by kids like us,
thinking they released some incredible key to our suffering.

If we were losing ourselves—getting by
with the new truths of our small lives
which we and the world would meet each day,

we didn't know.

Our world asked for souls,
        and we paid with the weight of having lived.

GOSPEL WITH QUARREL AND HAPLESS PRAYER

Holy Sunday and I'm losing myself to God, singing and shaking
in my first Communion dress. At first I don't hear them fighting in the pews,

only the slight rise and fall of two bodies.
When my father struggles down my mother's right wrist, then the left,
                    she twists like a wind chime.
Hand over hand, they push and pull
                    as if lifting each other to be blessed.

• • •

They look small from where I stand on the altar.

I can see the buttons missing from my mother's red sweater,
        how the shoulder pads are uneven and wing-clipped
        as she fights from the inside out.

When she shoves herself away from my father, a familiar sound—
her bracelets jangle glints of tiny crosses over the broad archways.

The other children laugh when I release my hands to cover my ears

        because my mother's voice drops to the polished floor
        as though calling out in sleep, or falling.

Forty faces shift; even the priest turns around. His hand shakes above my head
        and everyone's watching everyone's wondering
            until the usher steps in to escort my mother away.

• • •

My mother's grief, germ-like and oblique, spreads through me in one long
sparking scar.

As she is taken away, her eyes stay buried beneath a swirl of dark hair.
She is tired. She is harmless.

My father chases her down the aisle. They don't think I can see them
turning and turning, drifting farther from me
as though I could cup them in my palms and close them in.

The pamphlet turned fans, the incense plumes slants
in the privacy of steepled hands—

• • •

if I had known how the days would splay and break I would have cried mercy.

• • •

Late spring and juniper berries sprawl
along the sidewalks of County Line Road.

Now early morning snow crowns the ridgelines,

claims the flatlands in scratches
and garlands the oaks behind St. Michael's like spliced dovetails.

Here is the beginning of a season holding its breath
for a sacrament that never reaches grace.
Here are all the stains in the glass where the light decays.

The saints' mouths glow in congregations of solitary flames.
　　My mother's sobs spin pearls in their shriven ears and we call it holy.
　　Their black eyes ache watching us grow sick, we are sick—

· · ·

When they are cast out to suffer themselves,
bells ring their seizures of mercy.

The marriage ends and I don't blame them.
Every spring since, the vulnerable parts of me change.

Now the saints have names—
　　all we ever did was slip from their sprouting hands.

DRAGON'S DEN

Saturday nights, my sister and I went to our mother's AA meetings.
It was a cabin edged right up against the road.

We stole ceramic mugs from the community kitchen and hid them all
under the orange tweed couch. We splayed arms like searchlights

along the undersides of the vending machine—there was no change,
no reaching out then pulling in. We never quit cramming our overalls

with sugar packets, or filling Styrofoam cups with warm water.
Like torchbearers we excused ourselves between the crossed legs

of shaky adults, asking God to intervene. And still, our lives became
unmanageable. We meant to be good with pain—hungry and amazed.

Once, my mother caught my arm, whispered, *This is the last time*, so I hid
in the bathroom, standing on the toilet, listening through the vent

as her voice cleared through the week's struggle to feed us, keep us safe
from relapse. When the weather warmed, we escaped to the creek,

avoiding the older girls with purses calling us *bitches*.
Crane flies twisted into webs as we set them on fire. As the sun

curved west, we crawled from the high weeds, from the fox trails
peeling burrs from our shirts. We ran into the lobby where our mother

would read to us from the bold print looking up at the split
scroll of twelve steps suspended ceiling to floor, rolling

with the open and close of doors like it was made of breath.
I'd see men around her and shoot them down, my fingers pulled

into a gun behind her skirt. Sometimes they'd smile at me. I'd pretend
to make gators with my hands instead but they knew what I meant.

FIRST COMMUNION AFTER-PARTY

At the center of a strip mall down Colfax,
      the pink facade of Casa Bonita rose
      eighty-five feet above the deserted lot.

Big clouds rolled overhead, scudded east.
      It was the castle I needed to believe in,
      standing in my church clothes midafternoon

as the faces of the red rocks, miles out, jutted forth
      from the earth like cocked carbines.
      The fake blue fountain sprayed into dry air,

flecked my skin. Outside, the world was darkening.
      But inside the family restaurant, I watched
      two divers at the top of a fake cliff, arms raised

above their heads before synchronizing themselves
      thirty feet into the water tanks below.
      They called it a lagoon. A deep dark place.

I wanted it to be real. I didn't know the difference.
      Plastic skulls glowed along walls. Wooden signs
      displayed gun fights and puppet shows.

My velvet shoes stomped over plastic underbrush.
      Past the arcades and pirate cave, I posed
      for a photo behind the rubber bars of a western jail.

My Communion dress draped lace over the barstool
      like tablecloth. My props: a bottle of rye whiskey
      hugged under my right arm like a doll,

black cowboy hat pulled to the rims of my glasses,
     an old Colt .45 quiet on my left thigh
     like I had something to protect.

ANGER MANAGEMENT

Even when all the doors stood open, only the chimes thwanged—
monster, daughter, monster, daughter.

My mother carried a cast iron skillet from our stove
and a baseball bat from the garage
out toward the lilacs in the backyard, where dog bones
bordered the buckthorns like ochre-tinged gems.

Then she dropped the skillet,
        gripped the bat and swung at the cast iron,
        lost her step and hit the dog bones too—

sent them spinning as though she struck the yard jaw loose.

I pushed my chair from the dinner table,
looked out the screen door into the yard.

Cottonwoods spit seeds all along the eastern side
        of the High Line canal and into the soccer field.
                Like shed galaxies they released above the powerlines

and confettied the chain-links so by dusk,
        the air was thick with signals and nothing felt safe.

Circling the skillet,
        my mother paced back and forth
        as though there was a decision to make,
                tipped the bat back toward our yellow-slatted house.

She yelled *Everybody out* and I knew she meant me.
I knew she called me into that silt-green backyard so I wouldn't forget I was hers.

I was slight and glassy eyed against that stillborn afternoon,
waded toward the dull shine swinging low circles, beckoning
                    Hush baby, come to mama. I didn't want to

fix myself spread-legged in a chatter of dandelions
with my father's bat raised over my head.
Last apprentice to her grief. Girl in the racket of being there.

My mother nudged me forward and my small muscles flexed.
            My heart collapsed in my ears.

I lost control of myself until the swinging stopped
and I didn't remember my father's bat in my hands,

how I could have let go but didn't.
            I missed the skillet every time.

VISITING THE COLUMBINE MEMORIAL

The day Bill Clinton came to greet the grieving families,
        Columbine whistled behind banks
                of bare trees. School shut down.

Black SUVs formed single lines.
        Flags studded around the perimeter
                while a single helicopter circled above

floodlights bent toward the western summits.
        Ice cracking out on Bowles Lake like blanks.
                Runoff gurgled along the morning sod.

Across Littleton Boulevard, men in masks
        raised photographs of rifles—a few carried
                signs that read *Back Off* or *Gun Control Is Being Able*

to Hit Your Target. They warned those of us there to mourn
        that they were armed. They weren't going anywhere.
                The NRA convention downtown would go on as usual.

A few kept their hands stuffed deep within their pockets,
        said the two boys were sick in the head—
                It's not the guns, it's the people.

Ice hung from branches, weighed down grass.
        Everywhere we walked something broke.
                No one fought back, cars of the killed teenagers

opened like jars across the lawn, dropping
       stuffed animals, necklaces, handwritten cards.
              I didn't want to imagine what they said,

or who they belonged to.
       Other teenagers wore shirts that read
              I don't want to die. I didn't want to die.

Mounds of flowers scattered paths to the top
       of the highest hill where thirteen crosses
              plunged into the soft, wet ground.

CHILDREN ARE BURIED

Well past dawn, my sister and I
played on the concrete of the carport.

In beaded socks we jumped
through the air, our open jackets

flapping like flags. All morning,
we turned our bodies

against the far peaks beyond
the immediate visible world,

melting before we were born.
I held onto the basketball

as though praying, stayed
out there with wet hair,

sweat soaking through my palms
and fingers. Even in the late April

sun, snow spread over the ground,
packed high up under the pines

where grass refused to grow.
Reverbs of the ball knocked

the rim between stark shots
of car door slams up and down

the block. Lawns lined with faded flowers.
Newspapers filled with the same headlines.

Whole town briefly famous,
then forgotten.

One of the dead boys lived
five houses down. A week after

the shooting, funerals. Everywhere
we looked, dark cars slinked

along dripping edges of side streets.
Miles off, bells struggled

in the back gully of the canal.
Another victim's funeral.

Heads fixed in hands.
Coffee and casseroles shuttled

behind doors hammered
in wreaths. Shadows roamed

like dials, our feet left the ground,
our small muscles filled with blood

and the ball, cold from free throws
into old snow, slipped from our hands.

We didn't move as it spluttered
down the gutter, slick with leaves

melted raw by snowmelt, rolling
to a stop against a funeral goer's

shoes, limping through it all.

THE FIRST YEAR WE LIVED UNDERGROUND

During the wettest spring I've ever seen, we moved in with Uncle.
It was his first house, a chipped scab with a good yard. We ate from the apple trees
in the backyard, the gnarled branches bent with the wind. Bruised apples
pocked the ground that reeled out before us like shallow water pulling sand.

All our money was gone. That's how I understood it. My mother gave up
too much for us. And each night I thanked her, in my own quiet way.
I would never let her see that gratitude. I couldn't do that yet.

Then my mother stapled herself a room behind a survival blanket
slung from the ceiling in the back of the basement.
                        Helpless it hung and twisted like a thick veil.

Most nights, I heard my mother sigh behind that numb slur in the dark
like she just wanted some sun on her skin, and in the morning, I woke
to my mother's alarm that never stopped ringing.

I made stumbling to the blanket a habit.
I stood in the dark with my questions. The flow of her slow breathing
sounded like a slow tide trailing into the dark. I pulled the string for the light bulb.

Her bed was there, a nightstand, two lamps, her portable black-and-white TV.
Her night guard drifted like ghost shrimp across her pillow.
Wet petals bloomed from her mouth and she woke smiling, almost grateful.

Upstairs where I came up for air,
Uncle's posters of Elvis clung to the walls.
Each one, loyal and calm, made the house seem larger, more graceful.

All day the light came through. Cactus plants grew sharp as nerves
from the window glare. I liked it there.

The jeweled, mute versions of Elvis saved me,
dark eyes like life rafts gleamed but no songs sank into my flushed bones, no songs
                    in our separate rooms, no songs shook the house loose.

When the black lab dry-swallowed then spat back a piece of the King's acrylic face
I sat on the floor coloring the puzzle back in, wondering
                            what gave him the right to disappear.

And when the dog ran away for the last time, found dead along C-470,
Uncle was so lonely he painted his room blue.

For weeks, I heard howling in that room and I went back underground.
There was no outside world. Only the wet press of basement musk.

A blue void sunk in the storm drains and no one said a word,
our lips closed behind the veils we hung to keep ourselves asleep,
until we would each jolt back to life in the night to the sound of pacing rain,
                        disappearing, reappearing
each time louder, then farther away.

TRAIL DUST

The idea was to give corporate men
a new life. The entire steakhouse lined
with checkered picnic tables. Local
country bands played at the front stage

while my mother checked cowboy hats
at the door, turned them upside down,
the proper way, to avoid penny tips.
Every man wearing a tie had it cut

by a waitress like my mother who greeted
them with a pair of dull scissors.
They called my mother Six-Gun Sue,
refused to say her real name. She rattled

cowbells down the shotgun line of the banquet
hall for the ties that some men wore
just for that moment, to feel my mother's cool,
pale hand pulling them a little closer, to feel

her breath turn around their necks like mesh.
Walk in with a tie and it gets cut off without
warning. All ties hung to the walls in rows
like wet wildflowers, unfurled above crooked

pictures of old homesteads, the loneliness of this dry,
dusty earth caught endlessly swirling, the thin silver
frames such life contains, splashed with years
of forgotten stains. My mother would make

good money on those nights, but she had to play
the part—wore the heels, clothes southwestern
style. Under her slacks, a pair of five-pound
weights strapped around her ankles each night

she worked. I imagine she pushed her way
through the dance floor carrying trays
of iced tea in red glasses toward the threshold
of the back kitchen doors, shaped and cut

like the entrance of a saloon, legs red
with welts where the weight knocked
around her ankles, pulled on her skin.
Mouths moved over the loud music.

The weight of it all: heavy, as she asked
the busboys for more molly in the kitchens
to stay thin, and though I don't know
this world, I know its mangled need.

STAGE PRODUCTION

Years after the shooting, the local high schools
decided to merge our theaters together for a musical.
Columbine wanted to rebuild its reputation.
I stayed in the background, sang in the choir.

After a late rehearsal, one of the Columbine boys
gave a small group of the cast a tour of the school.
The whole place gutted. Fresh paint. New floor tiles.
Still in our stage makeup, we climbed the stairs

to the second floor in single file. Our blemishes
cracked beneath cheap concealer. Foundation split
at the hairline and temples. But I knew the stories—
students tripped through ruts to safety.

Palms clung to hunches of shoulders for stability,
made fistfuls of each other's clothes. Shoes wet
and smeared in ditch-mud. I had a babysitter
who married the person she escaped with, a coworker

now dependent on opiates, days of searching
for pills after surviving shots to the chest and head.
A girl in our group clutched a brass doorknob
to the utility closet where her brother packed in

with others, hid for hours and refused to open
the door, even for SWAT. Past the cafeteria,
where hard marble stairs began to the second floor,
I recognized the angled views from the security cameras

that played on the news, and I knew where I was.
At the top, I gripped the metal railing, palms pulsing.
On the other side of the cafeteria, a high wall of windows.
Late sun pierced down into the back lake, rearranged

stiff shallow waves. Faint light spread over wind-
ripped trees. Faded stars whirled overhead.
I was right there, with the teenagers in their world
shucked of its life, curled beneath the tables

and I tell you: I could feel it, the stroke of the gone.

DEFLECTION

Of all the epithets to come out of Jeffco—

      Goths and Gays,
             Gay Conspiracies to Kill Jocks,
Marilyn Manson,
           the Trench Coat Mafia,
white suburban gangs,
anyone who looked like the boys,
              or posed like them—
rejects touching in the hallways,
           group showering.
A sullen subculture known
           for dove-white face paint
and black clothes, lips, fingernails—
           dripping mascara;
           foil-heavy, tar-dark.
The stories were vague, second- and thirdhand.

        What became of me
           in those moments? At Clement Park,
the makeshift memorials
           grew so large, warehouses
were rented to store old letter jackets,
           beads, and ribbons. Crushed chimes
tore away the grass, dragged
           guttural, unfinished music
beneath thunderheads, dark as magazine clips.
           Rain like cold sweat.
For days the news reports droned on, searched
           for answers while blue and silver
balloons drifted over town.

CHARLIE BROWN'S

The bar was a wooden square, glasses upside down, chiming above heads
        where my mother and father drank Saturday nights. They were new
to Denver, cross of Mount Lindo high up in the dark. The broadcast signals
        driven into the buff rock of Lookout Mountain throbbed in the distance
over sage-crushed crossroads and little ranches where jagged basins flowed
        toward the city—you could see them for miles. Crusts of plaster littered
the landing of their apartment. Pantyhose and bras hung from shower rods.
        Books tented on an ironing board. They washed their hair in the sink.
Walked barefoot on loud floors that sloped. Charlie Brown's was a short
        walk down the road if you could manage the snow. It's still like that—
most people slide downhill into that piano bar from the streets, noses numb.
        Hard to imagine my parents drunk in song, leaning on each other.
My father can't sing, but I think he'd try. They were not ashamed.
        The sound of their laughter rose above soft sweeps of wind.

COLUMBINE

Now shredded clouds skirl
        beyond the foothills, aspens choke
the Swan River valley dredged for gold
        to its bedrock.
Magpies touch down on beetle-riven pines.
        No life for them here.
For months, rabbitbrush scrawls
        across what little snow scrolls the bluffs—
a record-breaking warm winter.
        The distance is constant.
Everything between brittle and heavy.
        Gnarled tree trunks twisted together.
Cobalt skies receding.
        In the stillness, sounds of Highway 9
waft up the mountainsides.
        Avalanche cannons explode, echo over scree.
And it clings to me, the wheel passing
        over spring. I sink into April like a spade,
brick-heavy, sputtering.
        Cusp of heaven crystallized, shatters
in the psyche of what happened here.
        We live with these deaths.
Old snow cinches each new leaf
        and does not let go.

CONDITIONS
OF THE
WOUNDED

CONDITIONS OF THE WOUNDED

She hurt inside. Her body suffered.
      Mornings she'd be at the edge of the bed, grasping

the small square of her T-shirt cinched in her fists, eyes wide.
      Not surprised her own lungs turned against her.

The doctors warned this could happen;
      the inwardness, the harm. If she had an asthma attack,

I roamed outside our red house, clattering against the range
      like a cold-burned star. I shot free throws

in my Valentine-studded dress,
      half-tucked into the hip of my white hose.

February snow thickened and thawed.
      Expanded, vanished. Five miles away, doctors

worked until her lungs sucked air back into my world.
      I carved chalk circles on the carport with sticks,

shot too far. Tossed my arms into the future
      around which our existence formed.

When she came home, cold light
      came in through the front door, wintry and wrought.

I watched dreams work twitches into the blue of her skin.
      Albuterol beside the bed like a bent, broken arm.

• • •

Even in dreams, loss was the author. My work was worry and wait.

• • •

She had 30 percent of the oxygen most people have,

said living felt like breathing through a straw.

When doctors strapped her into a wheelchair, she screamed.

Nothing I could do but scratch circles on the carport as ice ate away the roofs.

• • •

Age after age, time folds forward
        and the idea of my childhood

without my sister fades,
        becomes gray and visceral.

All my life,
        I wanted to know how to plot a course

through her threatening
        lungs. But if fear was a house,

it was ours. Absence of breath struck us down
        each heart-shaken day.

And all my life,
        we were consumed, learned to wear distress

like dresses tied around our waists
        and where buttons were missing, we clutched.

⋅ ⋅ ⋅

There was a time when my sister was a happy child.
She was happiest as a tomboy.

⋅ ⋅ ⋅

As teenagers, I mouthed

the words beneath my sister's

persistent harmonies.

In church, she was the loudest

soprano in the pew. Voice airy

and high. It was too much,

the weight of her, the surprise.

She scared me. Her voice harsh,

gasping even in hymns. Just know I sing

with her songs stuck in hand.

⋅ ⋅ ⋅

She was rebellious by then. Dinner, age sixteen, she threw an orange
    at my head.
I caught it. Bit into its skin and swallowed. I took anything
    she gave me seriously.

· · ·

During an asthma attack, the doctors
                        used the butterfly needle to draw blood.
The peak flow meter measured
                        her oxygen levels, forced into her mouth
on the third, fourth visit in a month. The doctors
                        ordered her to exhale as hard as she could and it hurt—
it should hurt, they said. For her, living
                        was like being choked from the inside.

· · ·

At home, the piano leg snapped.

The birdbath stacked on wet wood by the front windows
where the instrument chimed tones of dread without end.

When there was music
water rippled   when my sister sang   water rippled

and the gray jays came down but the keys went flat as fieldstones.
Handfuls of high-strung wires purred to no one but themselves.

It was the heaviest thing we owned.

· · ·

I return to these moments: the rage against herself,

the loosening of lungs failing, the words swelling

in the chest, her voice racing into my face.

Those nights she snuck out of the house, climbed through

the basement window, and vanished into the knee-scraping dark—

• • •

After college Jessie came home from the bar in a cab.

When she shrugged off her coat
                             it was as though she had diffusers

detonate from the inside.

As though she was pretending   we weren't there.

I thought I could see the liquor

                             working turns within the breath of her body.

Police summoned to our door, she never paid for the cab.

Our mother told us to stay inside,
                             stood on the mud-packed porch in whispers.

My sister moved behind me, squeezed my arms.

                             Her pink dress, faded as watercolor wash,

                             swished the backs of my knees.

• • •

Without her

I'm unhinged,
        de-winged, I tailspin

and won't leave.
        This shriek,

the scar and the suture,
my tangled shadow

        shook loose
from her silence, a mouth

in a veil of mud.

                                        • • •

By midwinter my sister didn't want to remember
        the drugs that made her slip too fast then toss

in lawless dreams. Her skin had always been pale,
        but now she woke lock-jawed. By the time she was nineteen

the piercings she had on the tongue, lip,
        nipples, and belly button made our mother cry.

One pulled the lower lip. The other weighed her tongue
        like an iron filling, a needle crushed through velvet.

                                        • • •

Again I lay awake and relive the memory:
the year we shared our mother's car
I was eighteen and my sister was twenty.
We had to refill the nebulizer machine
with albuterol. She lived in the city
and I drove from Littleton but my sister
was not at home. I found her instead
at a house in Five Points. Drunk
in the mineral-cold predawn, ice glowing
beneath her feet like fish bellies twisting
up from the ground. Her shadow flat on the ice,
she drowned in gravity. The sleet and gray
and waste of that day were all brutal.

• • •

I knew she was shit-faced in the salt of that bare-chested morning.
Barefoot, her black and gold coat howled wide open.
Around her snow fell a slumber of feathers.
Swayed on the pavement as though falling

into dream. Air clothed in steam and cold smoke.
Away from our city's rust and exhaust,
away from February's ice-slickened scalp,

her auburn hair uncoiled. In the cold,
I fussed with the soft tangles of her hair
and she slapped me. I tugged her pants

back up and she kicked me. We were going down
but side by side
we looked like amalgams, rewinding

years of crisscrossed hands, whirling
through patternless rooms because we liked the fear.

• • •

One gust-ridden and raw February, Jessie was kicked out
of her boyfriend's house for starting a fight. Taken out

of the house by two of his friends. Left in the street yelling
at the windows, stomping around in big boots. It was her birthday.

I was inside, strangers hoisting my ankles up for a keg stand.
Upside down, I could hear my sister's screams turn into ragged

sobs until she couldn't speak. The rest of me rotated as though pulled
from winter feetfirst. Her shouts, weakening. As though each time

she exhaled, ice hardened to her face. Lungs rattling against tarry
black. In the cold, I imagined her hands on her knees, plumes

of breath rising like smoke up through the night. All of the upright
parts of her crumbling. Breath, a torn wind. Her body ruined and still

her breath slowed to a choke, all of her shrinking.

• • •

Did not want to bear the world. Would not
        use the albuterol. Refused
        to take the medicine,
        left it stuffed in the farthest
        corner of the bathroom cabinet.

There was something in her that wanted to leave
        the fight against the regimen,
        something about the way dusk
        drowned its last grated edge
        in the valleys' shadows. She was done

with the swollen blue charts of lung capacities,
	the constant flinching
	in our household, her body
	thrashing. Mouth working
	without sound. I felt it in me too—

a soft-gummed drumming
	in the throat, a white seed
		set to spiral in the slow opening of a lung.

· · ·

We knew the song by heart.

· · ·

			I grabbed my keys and pulled her by the arm
			to the car, lowered her inside the passenger seat,

				closed the door, climbed behind the wheel
				and the world became me and her

					behind an icy bed of glass. We drove
					through the county line's broken curves,

					through sanctuaries of sloshing snow.
					Through the turning dust and railways,

				through the farmlands smell of sulfur and soil,
				we passed the dry grass and ice-melt needling

				along the ditches near Columbine. We smelled
				the ponderosas and starts of dandelion heads

set to bloom in the meridians. Seemed ours was the only
car, that there were no houses for miles, just snow

packed in, ringing like bullet shells toward
the doctor's office to where we would beg for more albuterol.

• • •

The doctors knew she was coming. Still drunk, she wrestled me to the ground
in the parking lot. Out of spit and dust,
from ache and spins my sister and I
scratched, all elbows and wrists. Scrapes on our arms left us striped.
All of it distilled to one soft-sided breath
scalding air, scaling sky.

• • •

There are places I can't go. She's in all of them.

LIVING
FROM
THE
INSIDE
OUT

SEVERAL DEATHS OF MY SISTER

1

She is born half-crushed, trawling with a hip brace
through the house grasping counters, pulling herself up
        until she catches in the morning's white gleam
and watches the mountains in the windows striate her throat
and when their rocks fall, it is no accident they deaden in my hands.

2

She backs into a cactus and I try to pull her out
        before she breaks through the cradled scatter
but she wants to stay; to move makes it worse. I know she's right.

                I stare and yell and she cries into the sun.

3

She's in the bathroom and breathes hard
at night when the air closes like a muffled rag.

Sometimes I use her inhalers to flinch back what little survives
        and wheeze her name in front of the mirror
            becoming a lesser version of myself, a shattered camouflage
in all the cutting views and all the gliding light.

4

I am at the top of the stairs looking down
from where she falls, and she does not get up
            until I ask her to.

5

What I remember: cuts on her arms like chine
                deep ravines making herself beautiful and she means it—
the welts rise until skin swells and I take what I see. I turn away

and razors petrify what the light did not do, cauterize the wound
with a single lash—yes,
I've been willing to wage her ransom in dirge

so how is she not dead,

why not punish the hurt from ourselves, why not the sisterless fear,
why not the tendency to assume the worst?

6

Because I can't bring her back once she leaves
she is thirsty for relief that never arrives
                because she hobbles from doors when things go wrong
because she sings in the window propped on the hutch
because she can't stand huffing the dust of us—

7

she goes on dying,

        changes her name, hits bottom and is born again
on the wrong side of the river that only rises when she's lonely
                pulling mud from her throat
trying to cross her name,
a slur of words thrumming from my mouth and I cannot say anything,
    just hum—

the firstborn is a body willing to break all that's breaking through.

WE WERE RAISED ON ALERT

someone set the elementary school on fire
and months after, a fourth grader was found with a knife

at school, said it kept him safe.
Junior year, the year I fell in love with being wasted,

a classmate lit incense in his locker
and the state called SWAT to secure the bomb threat.

Hard to live in Colorado if you know it well.
Time never soothed our grief, but the weed did.

Getting high was easy. Except when I'd rip bongs
too hard then watch from the backs of my eyes,

dry as drought, the speck-grained images
from so many years ago of girls like me running from the school.

I lost myself in that place, became
the girl on the couch, memorizing my route. *Fuck the world*

and let's get high was our creed. We sang
it like a pledge. Beneath our shirts, we gleamed with our cannabis

belly button rings. I wanted it to last forever.
I've spent most of my life that way, adapting to a tight situation.

Became a cheerleader, or a target, wore
the skirts in math class and screamed during basketball games, absent

of my own suffering. We were scared
of each other. Stayed scared, would never admit our fear, thinking

we were too old to be afraid. Not surviving high school
was in all my dreams. I was paranoid and prepared.

Huddled there in a loose circle, fidgeting
for the announcer's grown voice to shout *Littleton High,* our ribbons

leaped in front of our faces,
ponytails curled around shoulders; we straightened

our matching socks woven
in purple thread and thought we had it figured out.

Soon we would clap and bend ourselves into splits,
holding on for life until the judges decided if our spirit proved strong.

All year, we smeared Vaseline on our teeth to keep smiling.

EVERGREEN MOTEL

And so it became an experiment, lying
to the saleswoman behind the Clinique booth
in the Park Meadows Mall. I was meeting

my boyfriend's parents for the first time
and needed the smoky eye—she believed me.
After she smudged silver streaks then blew

across my lids, swollen as baby rattlers, lulling
like dull bulbs down the county line, storms
splayed blue-footed over the eastern plains,

opening all the mischief in my heart
in want of release. Children came home
from school and I wore the skin of ecstasy.

The photographer kept the curtains shut,
his first rule. No beer, no weed. Metal bed
folded into a gurney. Under my clothes,

some unbelonging heaven shot
from my knees, girl-light from a lonely dream.
In my sister's lingerie, I braved the sorrow-

strewn world bleating into me. The photographer
brushed my hair. I let him brush my hair.
Between shudders, between each twirl of hair,

a stunned sun; the lens, wink-wallowed
flashes throning myself blind to glare.
Nobody knew where I went those days.

The crawl of my body was sentinel,
acting out commands like catalogs
of backward glances toward the places

I'd never return. I yearned to be seen,
that much was true. Wanted out of Littleton
so bad I shed clothes, the halter tops

and short shorts separating me from grace.
Over the ranch houses, thunderheads
sank into blond grasslands, drifting

as far west as Nevada. The camera
came down, curtains stayed shut
and the photographer's hands dove

through my hair, wound into the braids
of my pigtails, pulling me closer.
I can tell you now I felt it for days.

TO THE WOMAN IN WITHDRAWAL
NEXT COT OVER AT THE DENVER FACILITY
FOR PUBLIC INEBRIATES

It's time to admit I tried to forget
the way you fell to the ground

in shakes, how you hauled yourself
toward me by your forearms after rolling

from your cot, so slow and unbelievable
I didn't move, couldn't—honest to God,

I wanted to see you make it to whatever
asylum burst past the thought of sleep.

After all these years I can still hear
you inching across the linoleum floor

before your right leg angled over the mesh
of my cot and began kicking my legs and back.

All this time and it comes back like this:
your wrecked face in my hands pushing

down. Your wet grip on my wrists
like a wheel. How the fluorescents burned

mirages behind my eyes and failed me too.
As one patient continued to nod off, unable

to rise from the spins, another bathed naked
in toilet water, blue washrag spun to the top

of her head like a horn. It was winter.
Outside, snowplows slashed slow paths.

The nurses must have heard our struggle
over the drones of their TV. They came

running from behind the pale curtains
and found us wrestling down the paper

blankets. It took three of them to pry us
apart, to press you back into your cot

as though laying a brick. All I did
was watch, my back sealed to the orange

wall, shirt sideways, five hours into detox,
your wails breaking across dawn.

NO DAUGHTER IN THE BLEACHERS

Our apartment was separated from the sedge-thick
ball field by a creek where each weekend, I leaned
from the balcony watching my father run bases.
I heard echoes of men across slow-moving water.

I could see the high school and past that, jags of mountains
curled behind the dugout surrounded by needle-bare pines.
He was playing shortstop when he sprained his groin.
For weeks, straddled ice packs around his upper thighs

like a diaper. Years later, when he slammed into the left fielder
catching a mishit just over the infield, I was selling beer,
my third season at Coors Field. No one called
each other's name, no one claimed what descended

upon them like age. Just grown men low in the field,
gloves pawing air as though beating back flames.
After a doubleheader at the ballpark downtown,
I crossed home plate, our third-floor doorstep,

and saw my shirtless father at the table, his right arm
hooked in a sling he made from his undershirt.
He stood when I shut the door. I was used to the injuries.
My name tag was loose, jersey blotched with mustard

and booze. We both reeked. That night, I watched videos
of shoulder surgeries. The Rockies were playing the Diamondbacks
in Phoenix. No other work for me but this: the doctors let me
say good-bye before my father went under. Next morning,

he was blanketed, a man in a landscape of sails.
Maybe I tried to touch him. Maybe I said *See you soon*
or *Don't flirt with the nurses*, or *do*. I didn't want him to be alone,
I didn't want to be the only woman in the apartment anymore.

After open-shoulder surgery, he was behind a shower curtain.
A machine helped him move as though learning to swim.
Then it fell to me: lift and dress. Obedience, my vocation
until I was part of it too, rocking in the gestures of pain,

hanging on and letting go. I managed my father
back into his jersey. He was number 7,
half-dressed out the hospital doors and into the sun-
torn dust of July. His shirt was unbuttoned;

bare-chested, pieces of gauze stuck in his arm hair. Belt low
to the belly, pants undone. He threw up on me, hands tangled
in my shirt. I swallowed what awful thing I could have said
but wouldn't. There wasn't much to do but let it happen,

the weight of him slipping through my hands, his heavy
drop to pavement. No real choice but to embrace
his off-kilter body—I was learning to love the bent
creature he became. In our apartment, I motioned his arm

into a new sling, hooked him up to the TENS machine.
He was propped in the La-Z-Boy against the sliding glass door
to the balcony where the still-muddied marble of the diamond
lay just beyond the shimmering creek and chain-link outside.

My father sat hunched over his green beans, head low,
cartoons on the TV far off as though playing from a dream.
The mantle deep with trophies and slashed signatures
along baseball seams. He liked to sleep in his underwear.

He was like a son—clothes off for days while ice packs
burned his skin; a test for myself with the crying boy
of my father. He fell asleep looking out the window,
the unhurt parts of him twitching, trying to make right

the newly cut tendon, shaved shoulder blade, and suture.
His mouth was open, neck rigid with the labor of sleep.
When cracks of distant ground balls woke him, he stood
and stared. He heard his pain out there. At night,

the diamond outside widened in bone-light like a frozen lake.
Milk pods rolled in fly-blown winds, scattered through dry
reeds like flint. Always, I was afraid someone would see
my father half-naked in the moonlight like a ghost boy.

From one side of my life to the next, those blue
mountains behind our apartment looked as though
they could move. They never did. Before sleep,
I smothered lotion on my father's chapped back,

watching the peaks darken then flicker with light
shimmering from higher elevations. Touched him
like this: barely at all, only with the palms,
kept my fingers up. When it was over, I moved on

to the next task to stay busy, not because I wanted to
or should have but because I knew the hurt—
his helmet spinning like a bowl in dirt.
The last pitch gaining speed before striking down.

LATE IN THE PLAYOFF SEASON

After running past portable bleachers
and jumbo freezers of crushed ice

for the concession stands, I threw
my backpack under the linen shelves

in the kitchens, pulled on my unwashed jersey
and filled each cup holder in my section

with paper menus—nine dollars for hot dogs,
twelve for nachos. Then poured myself a drink

behind the bar, walked outside to my section
behind home plate and sat down in row 4, seat 7.

Organ chords blared through the grandstands.
Behind third base, González and Herrera

clutched the practice cage where fouls fell
toward a long band of mountains

stretched in the distance beneath a giant neon
baseball. I let the alcohol swelter through my body.

Cleats on concrete paced the dugout.
Sometimes I ate popcorn, waiting

for a hitter to knock the batting doughnut
off his bat in the on-deck circle before I went back

inside. Waitresses were smuggling muffins
and melon balls wrapped in napkins

into their pockets. By the first homerun
of the day, I took to comping drinks for my section

and kept them stashed in the inventory closet,
drank by myself behind boxes of liquid soft serve

and buffet tongs. During the fifth or sixth inning,
when the umpires convened in the clubhouse corridors

over at-bats and line drives, I held my tray
to my chest, made room so they could pass

in single file back to the field,
faces frowned with imagined called outs.

The broadcast cameras turned like cranes
and I'd be on TV, swaying

in my mesh jersey, streaked in relish and beer.
So drunk by last call,

I was barely able to close out my section,
delivering drinks floundering

with my tray as though it were a wide jaw.
Before I clocked out, if I clocked out at all,

I filled a paper cup with whiskey behind the bar,
said it was for a season-ticket holder, and left

by the seventh-inning stretch, stumbling
toward the I-70 underpass just as the evening sax

solos began bebops. It was as though I fell
asleep and let the darkness in the low sky pass

through the sockets in my skull.
As though all that fell before my eyes was specter,

a flag draped over my life's inner workings.
After my shifts, I'd wake in my work clothes

not knowing what hour or day it was,
apron slumped around my knees

remembering how my hands scanned the house walls
to where my mother's door met mine—

my mother's car on the lawn;
the pale hull of it, an ending itself.

THE DIAMOND CABARET

I didn't go home,
                 never turned my mother's car west

toward the Rio Grande shuffling south
                 toward the sandstones of Grand Junction

to end up in the front yard,
                 but followed a party into one of the many bars

or a strip club where I lived a different life than my own.
                 In this place, women spun flips on what seemed

like liquid discs floating on dark water.
                 The floor was a black galaxy

of scuffed streaks, while at the main stage,
                 a girl rotated against pink curtains.

Never mind how I stood there in the bad air
                 wanting it to be me stripped bare, deafened

by the hot wasting of need.
                 The rap so loud and I so drunk

I could barely feel myself float
                 between sequined arms, too gone to notice

the shimmering boas wrapped around my neck
                 like leashes. I didn't know where I was,

or how I got there. But the dances—
                    I studied everything. Became more aware

of the mechanics within my legs
                    and neck, fearing my life

without love. I stood in a pool
                    of light spilling from the stage, body heavy and sore

from lifting trays of beer over my head
                    all day. I drank as much as I could

until music stopped playing and the lights
                    came up. Late evening,

I would stumble through the blacked-out doors
                    into the street where the burnt arc of sun

curved low behind the farthest peaks.
                    The mountains suddenly graphite.

That was west; I hugged that darkening rim
                    south and I was home until the one day I didn't—

the one day I unstrung the boas and left the club
                    with bass lines still breaking behind my skull.

Cool smell of watermelons and Marlboros.
                    My mother's Volvo parked at the last meter.

Keys warm in my apron pocket.
                    Construction. Directions I couldn't follow,

single lanes, an officer approaching cars
        at the stoplight gesturing reroutes.

He smelled the booze on me, spilled beer from work,
        heard my slurred speech. My breathing, irregular.

My mouth corkscrewed instead of smiled, swaying
        with finger on nose, arms kinked

as though learning to walk with my hips
        for the first time. His palms crushed my wrists,

pushed my head into the vacant threshold of his car.
        As we pulled away from the city limits,

he said I should know how much
        I looked like his daughter. Hands cuffed

behind my back, I watched Denver flicker past.
        But I already lived from the inside out, spinning

in the flotsam of a darkness so absolute
        I couldn't deliver myself from it if I tried.

COURT HEARING

My lawyer ran through the usual questions,
     what I drank and how long was I in custody—
          what did I blow? Did I even remember?

He wrote a few answers of his own on a notepad.
     Something of potential. Such promise: a girl
          from a town where the dead stay young,

can't stand the dirt, twist their wrists into the earth
     when the living come around.
          As I approached the lectern,

a woman had already lost custody
     of her sons, didn't know which exit to use.
          Brothers were escorted away in cuffs

to their new lives in jail. Fourth, fifth offenders.
     Strings of metal jays were installed
          in the courthouse lobby; they swung

and crashed into each other beneath
     the sound of drills. Time slowed and dilated,
          one year for my life to spread a dull reel.

My hair hung in damp curls. Lips dry,
     stuck together. I could feel everyone's stares,
          felt skinned. I was told to plead. Went inward,

asked for oblivion. For years I drove drunk
     with fifths and six-packs in the passenger seat,
          yelling out the window to anyone.

It was all true. The courthouse was full.
>My mother watched from the back bench
>>with her gloves still on, shaking her head side to side.

My lawyer asked to approach the bench.
>I couldn't feel my legs but knew
>>I was standing, aware of my exposed feet

in open-toed shoes. Words passed
>between the two men, but I couldn't make
>>them out. Seemed to me whatever

the judge said, the lawyer hummed back.
>The room filled with strangers.
>>Babies lulled in carriers, no playing allowed.

Finally, the men were done.
>People became numbers. Lives
>>more important than mine, wrecked.

I was guilty. Reckless
>to say it straight up, to call it toward me,
>>to make known. And my mother,

woman in the back bench—
>what did you see? What reached your ear,
>>swelled on the seal of your tongue?

ANGER MANAGEMENT

1

Weeknights I shuffled in mustard-stained shoes
from the bus to the Speed Queen laundromat.

Second floor up was a dance studio.
On the paper sign at the base of the stairs
two silhouettes spun locked in arms.

At the top of the staircase the behavior facility
chimed with wall clocks. Elevator broken since August.
No door. It looked more like an unfinished closet.

Coffee makers that didn't work, couches
stacked on each other in the corners.
Carpet poorly pulled and stapled in places.

Furniture arranged in close circles.
Cigarette smoke almost clouded over
the rotting milk and vegetables in the refrigerator.

Thirty dollars each session. Up front. Cash only.
Any given night there were ten to fifteen offenders.
Depending on the relapses, bus schedules.

Some repeats. Some so new they came straight from court.
A black-and-white poster of Reagan bowling
hung above us all. Typed prayers taped to the walls.

A picture of a pregnant woman cradling
her unborn against a desert sunset
was the closest thing there was to a window.

Session after session, we discussed relaxation skills.
Practiced thought replacement, eye contact.
Anger is the biggest threat of self-control, we echoed.

Then waited for our own voices to calm ourselves.
Made friends with our triggers, used "I" messages—
I am feeling angry. I am mad.

2

Every night, we created anger ladders:
red in the face, rapid breathing, fast heartbeat,
thoughts of being short changed, restless.

The more we opened up, the more check marks
on our worksheets. When the pens didn't work,
we got stickers. Foul language never tolerated.

Bad attitudes never tolerated.
One day a guy came in with a high-risk situation,
said he stepped out onto what he thought

was his twenty-third-floor balcony
to jump. Found peace in the thought.
Stripped himself naked in the early January dawn.

But he was too drunk to remember he lived
on the ground floor. He fell three feet into the snow,
the cold—stinging flames. Not until a neighbor

found him and called the police
did he wake to the awful news he was still alive.
We scanned each other for the inner rustles

of our rage, filling in the blank gaps
that loomed in our minds. Let me explain:
our anger wasn't defined by the severity

of our punishment but by what we lost
in the process. First went hope, then control.
I wasn't surprised by the story; I survived myself too.

That's what was said. That's what we believed.

COMMUNITY SERVICE AT THE
LITTLETON HISTORICAL MUSEUM

Inside the collections center, life-size dioramas
of Littleton's history blink on and off.

What vanishes reappears.

In all corners of the room, I step into another time.
Easy to think I'm seeing the world
as it was before me. If I could push through
the glass and emerge on the other side,
I would see myself swinging in the cottonwoods as a child.

The front range spread jagged as blue hatchets.

But I take my time, let myself breathe
against the margins of these otherworlds;

      the southwestern ghost-town atlases,
      a galvanized cupola from the barn near Bowles Lake,
      deeds to the Rough and Ready Flour Mill,
      freight tariffs when the Denver and Rio Grande
      railroad pursued the Pike's Peak gold rush boom.

Days like today, high spruces lurch above the farms.

High pitches of hymns sound behind the mule sheds.
Nuns in the convent down the road
               sing through the trees.

The bells ring and I can't listen to anything else.
               Not even allowed to talk.

Even when the children tug on my coat, gesturing
toward the mud-slathered pigs, I turn away. They wave,

                    and I nod. I asked for this.

Peacocks shoved off the sidewalks with a broom,
matches I light in the janitor's closet, ripping

cobwebs down from corridors. Ammonia sloshes
in a bucket as I polish the cubby holes in the playroom

where, as a child, I used to set fake tables
                        for a family that wasn't mine.

For a moment I forget it's a punishment.

When the pastures thicken with children, mud
tunnels through on their shoes and I scrub
weathered sideboards with a toothbrush.

They run back and forth from the old school-
house situated way out there like a nub, coal stove
lifting up wheat shocks of smoke over the stubble fields.

From the east side of Gallup Reservoir,
thin snow limns the ends of wooden planks.

It's been months beneath this cold-burned curve of sky.

Days clearing shit from the barns, rose-skulled
slush seeps in my shoes. That's about all I do.

I've swept myself into a corner here

MOTHERS AGAINST DRUNK DRIVING

A slideshow of the dead played on loop from the stage.

Teenagers with bodies grown awkward by hormones,
thick hair gel clumped through clouds of hair. All clean
eyes and teeth. There was nothing else to look at.

Men in Dickies pants stretched their legs.
Women released hard work from their braids.
Arms crossed over stomachs. Necks snapped and set.
Bandanas pulled tight around heads.

Phones tucked deep into socks, otherwise the police
locked them in the janitor's closet down the hall.
If we spoke, our probation officers got a phone call.

With the lights out, the victims brightened the overhead screen.
Before the panel even began, interludes of slow music played.

Once my eyes adjusted to the dark,
I tried to figure out where it was coming from.

Some of us had become so used to sitting still,
we knew how to let punishment pass
over as easily as pulling a sheet over our heads.

To save ourselves, we had to hear it:
a woman in a white pantsuit sang at the back of the house.

We listened, a melody spiraling out into the infinite dusk.
Some refused to look. Seemed like she was moving down clouds.
She was the pull of gravity itself.

Whatever she touched slumped.

Some of us turned to watch her gliding
like a figure skater from the edges of our sight line.

She walked and sang between us in the dark,
studied our faces, then climbed stage left.

When her song was over, she turned around,
hands up to strike, the grief deepening its hold.

Every time she sang from those stairs,
she saw a version of her son that was alive.

I wondered if by being there, we were making it worse.
I wondered when she looked down and saw me sitting there,
if she understood how I was just a breath
held inside my own sorry mouth.

Then other women walked on stage
wearing matching shirts with the letters *M.A.D.D.*
slashed in thick red lines.

In collapsible chairs they held themselves
apart, all of us trying to defy our own tragedies.

The mothers didn't rush for us down rows of slouched sweatshirts.

They were calm, and their calm was proof
their children were real,
as though all they heard were radiators
still hissing into ruts; it was us.

The dead flickered and faded above us all.

I lurched with the dirty ache, held my head up with my fists.
My jaw clicked and grinded.

One mother doubled in her chair, eyes closed.
A group of three held hands beneath the table,
held each other's fists up in encouragement.

All I could do was daydream, how the pines swayed while dying.
Flustered while eaten alive from the inside.

They made a lesson of me, said I was young enough to be on that screen.
What could I have killed?

The singer—she watched me the whole time,
read my thoughts, knew what I wanted to say but didn't.

Her son was gone and my own mother waited
outside the school in the cold of the Volvo, staring
at stars blinking on and off over the parking lot.

LANDSCAPE ON THE 38TH DAY OF PROBATION

If I missed one day at the Whiz Quiz,
        time hung to my sentence.

Didn't know when, but three times a month,
        my number was called

and I stiffened in the wind, willows lashing
        everywhere I went, path scratched

long by a lean sun. It was too far to anything—
        my ten-speed sunk in slushed snow and salty melt.

Midwinter left a whiteout through the neighborhood,
        finches patrolled jagged stumps beside a landfill

with a sign *coyote area*: the warnings warped
        or plowed down from drunk drivers

after dark in places like Arapahoe County
        whose laborers shared too many pitchers, hugged

edges of trail turnoffs, and woke
        inside red-beaked dawn, hoods ticking.

The Highline Canal was a dry ditch.
        My tread left a pattern like bandages,

spreading behind me, lingering
        barely a forethought in the memory

of the facility manager who looked out
                and saw my glittered spokes kicking snow

into the trench light of the canal. Icicles fell,
                became currents. From frozen ground, raw oaks

sank anchored, bark blistered, hollow.
                Streamers blew out from the handlebars,

whipped my wrists. Clothes hard and loud.
                Sky smeared a pearly calm and under it,

my bellowing into the open folds
                of my coat, hating how it made me warm.

MONITORED SOBRIETY

There was a routine: I rang the probation line
every morning at six. Never had an answer
for why my probation officer called me Phil;

maybe it was easier to remember me as a man.
Whatever the reason, when his machine asked
for Phil, it was my pissing day.

Impossible to pay rent so I lived in the third-floor
apartment with my father. Wasn't allowed to drive
so I took his car. The keys spread on his dresser

by the Oscar Wilde whistle and photo of the 1994
Rockies opener, Dante Bichette's arms wrapped
around my sister and my sunburned shoulders.

Early as morning pastures shocked geese to splotch
the purpling range, my father slept beneath
an American flag in his boxers, snoring

with a bent nose strip dangling from the edge
of his nose. Humidifier steamed stale air.

In the cold dark, when sunup blazed
the sides of Evergreen Point Apartments, stripped
and ice laced, I swirled a pocket of frost over the dash

with my sleeve and slipped into the driver's seat.
Inside the facility, the employees were already high,
hallways blue with smoke like diving to the bottom

of a lake turned suddenly warm. I knew all of them
by name, never spoke. How the air around them soured
and staled. Others leaned over the counter and yelled

my name, made jokes I didn't have the answer for.
Of course they did; little else happened in Littleton anymore.
A few benches and tables set up with clipboards.

As I handed over forty dollars for the test,
the clerk pulled a wad of cash from his pocket,
added mine, started counting. Bathroom stripped of a door.

The officer's eyes stayed on me while I crouched,
promising there was no recent use of alcohol,
bath salts, spice, marijuana, cold medicines—

none of it. No drugs up my ass or in my jeans.
He scratched something on a clipboard. The clerk
licked a finger, parted bills, bowed into his grin.

COMMODITY

Sun-washed tumbleweeds swept past the donation center
where I sold my plasma to pay the probation fees. No more
than three visits a month or the nausea swirled and somersaulted.
Twenty-five dollars each time. Lightheaded with my shirtsleeve
rolled past the deltoid, a green spaceship Band-Aid slapped tight
against my skin, slapped again by an infant I promised to hold
until the mother, pressed into a vinyl chair as though sleeping,
was comfortable—thin line of blood surging above and behind
her head into fat bags. I danced and rocked the baby in front
of dust-crazed windows. Focused on nothing but sky and trailers
and great sweeping fields, the little open land left out to where
the airport leaned into a fuchsia horizon like a circus tent.
Behind me, needles pushed into arms one at a time.

AFTERMATH

ESCAPE PLANS

Every August, I scan each new classroom for windows I could break.
Which hallways are more accessible. Then maybe how, later on
in the semester, I'll start to notice the impulses of my own students.
Which ones are at-risk. Which ones I believe could kill me.
The answer is all of them. I don't say I feel hunted or that I've been
ready for the worst. My students catch me staring
out the windows and I don't tell them I'm looking for the thickest trees
for the widest width. Which ones could catch the most bullets.
How I imagine flipping up all the tables and chairs. What objects,
if any, are available for a blockade. There are days I can't leave
my office when I have to. I force myself into the classroom anyway.
Take my chances. Students run in the halls and I freeze. Keys ready
after class, I can't open doors fast enough. Every day is a protest
against someone who wants me dead. These bookshelves are my best
buffer. But I wouldn't upturn my desk, wouldn't make objects
into a shield or shell because that would be a mistake. I've thought
of everything. It's a long drop down, but I would jump.

AFTERMATH

I have tried to say this other ways—
      we were damaged. Cold mountain mornings,
         broken branches trembled in our drowsy air.

Sagebrush washed through the fence lines.
      The canal curved flat, power lines dissected
         chicory-ripe ridges. Our plum tree swayed

heavy in the wind. Outside the house,
      swollen bulbs in the ground stunned suddenly
         open, corrosive with lethargy. My eyes,

sun-withered wicks, squinted behind half-drawn curtains.
      Hard to stay out of the dark, isn't it? What does
         it matter what held me, or who,

but the ghost of the lost and gone? Each day,
      my life begins. Crabapples spatter the ravine.
         Towhees scream and I've become so used

to that sound, another sharp heart in the yard's stark tune.
      This time it isn't the rest of the raptured earth
         I hear but myself, yearning this way.

Always seems what I wanted to be true about heartache
      isn't. There is no bullet-worthy clemency. It knows
         no ease. I can sense it—absence, its tunneling

of the body; a grief I learned to live through by not
      remembering whole days. It gets easier, is what
         I mean. What a lie it'd be to say every shooting

no longer shakes me from dreams, awake
      and heaving, splashed in my own vomit. Takes
         all but dying to slip from my skin, to calm

the beating between the ribs. The only world I knew—
      mountains, the blur of light and shadow from Evans,
         Quandary, those ice-gutted glaciers letting go—

is not the same country I see leaning over
      these fences, split-pitch pine awash in June grass,
         lodgepoles pulled to the ground

like half-sunk tusks, but it's the closest I can get to a home
      anymore. I'm still living behind a meadow, studying
         the shape of snowcaps. Cone-heavy fir trees rock

on the face of the creek, needles split like hairpins
      in the ditch weed. Over and beyond, the mountains
         never move; they stay where they are

and never move. Only weak haze drifts across
      them now, faint and thin; violet streaks reach
         across frozen skies. Shouts fill the dugouts.

Cleats in the fields clutch and run through mud and past
      the chain-link, the ranges spread on forever. Magenta
         wounds. The rage in us blistering.

Flag half-mast at the high school. Just cottonwoods forever
         then evergreens. Above tree line, bristlecones torque
                  into themselves, petrified. Starts of wet flakes

wield outward. End the drifting for miles down
         these hills. Send me down, spin me in all directions.
                  This is one way of accepting the life I've inherited—

let the dead dream along the churning edges of earth.
All the surprises ahead of me I already know.

ACKNOWLEDGMENTS

I am grateful to the editors and staff of the following publications where the poems in this book first appeared:

Blackbird: "Aftermath," "Escape Plans," "On Lockdown"
Hunger Mountain: "Children Are Buried," "Visiting the Columbine Memorial"
Indiana Review: "The First Year We Lived Underground"
Memorious: "Gospel with Quarrel and Hapless Prayer"
Missouri Review (online): "Several Deaths of My Sister"
Poetry Northwest: "Burying the Time Capsule at Dark Not Long after the
    Columbine High School Shooting"
RHINO: "To the Woman in Withdrawal Next Cot over at the Denver Facility
    for Public Inebriates"
Salt Hill Journal: "The Bomb Shelter"
Sou'Wester: "Anger Management," "Monitored Sobriety"
Thrush Poetry Journal: "Dragon's Den"

. . .

"Stage Production" was first published in *Bullets into Bells: Poets & Citizens Respond to Gun Violence*.

"To the Woman in Withdrawal Next Cot over at the Denver Facility for Public Inebriates" was selected for an Illinois Arts Council Agency Award.

Acknowledgment is due to the following for their support: Southern Illinois University–Carbondale and University of Colorado–Denver. My immense gratitude to my fellow writers and poets for the keen eyes and support in the time before, during, and after writing these poems: Judy Jordan, Allison Joseph, Jon Tribble, Jake Adam York, Teresa Dzieglewicz, Meghann Plunkett, Andrew Hemmert, James Dunlap, John McCarthy, and Jacqui Zeng.

This book could not have been finished without support from my mother, father, and sister. Their trust, love, and generosity of spirit were the final stitching.

Lastly, to the person who motivates me to keep going, Graham Brewer, thank you.

Wisconsin Poetry Series

Edited by Ronald Wallace and Sean Bishop

(B) = Winner of the Brittingham Prize in Poetry

(FP) = Winner of the Felix Pollak Prize in Poetry

(4L) = Winner of the Four Lakes Prize in Poetry